THE CHILDREN'S LIBRARY

VOLUME THREE

STORIES FROM FAIRYLAND

THE CHILDREN'S LIBRARY.

THE BROWN OWL.
THE CHINA CUP, AND OTHER STORIES.
STORIES FROM FAIRYLAND.
THE LITTLE PRINCESS.
PINOCCHIO THE PUPPET.
IRISH FAIRY TALES.

(Others in the Press.)

THE WINGS OF THE SOUL.

STORIES
FROM
FAIRYLAND

BY
GEORGE DROSINES

AND

THE CUP OF TEARS
AND OTHER TALES
BY ARISTOTLE KOURTIDOS

TRANSLATED FROM THE GREEK
BY
MRS. EDMONDS

LONDON
T. FISHER UNWIN
1892

PREFACE

HE title of 'Stories from Fairyland,' which is here given to the following translations of short stories from George Drosines, may be objected to by those who know the originals as not being the equivalent of the Greek word Παραμύθια. It is not, however, put forth as an English rendering of the word. Moreover, there are no fairies in Greece; those mythic creations so much beloved of us

belong almost exclusively to our race. Greece has her Nereids, which, so far as attractive loveliness is concerned, may be said to resemble our fairies, but are nevertheless essentially different, as they are generally more disposed to allure to their destruction rather than to benefit those of the human race who are fascinated by their beauty.

There are, however, in the charming tale of 'The Maiden's Three Gifts' all the conditions of a true and genuine fairy tale. Notwithstanding that the three visitants who came to endow the new-born babe on account of its beauty are called 'Μοῖραι,' and notwithstanding the significant number *three*, they are in no wise analogous to the three Fates of archaic mythology, but are essentially *good fairies*, and their mission, by rendering the word Μοῖραι 'fairies,' becomes intelligible to us.

From this one story alone, which supplies all the proper requisites, without any reference to others, I feel myself justified in calling them Stories from Fairyland.

E. M. EDMONDS.

CONTENTS

	PAGE
A Grandfather's Story	1
The Maiden's Three Gifts	13
The Musician and the Dancer	25
The Cousin of the Rose	34
The Death of the Poppy	39
The Wings of the Soul	44
The Cuckoo Clock	51
The Rook's Bath	55
The Mother's Blessing	59
The Foolish Cricket	70
The Two Snails	73
The Enchanted Fountain	77

CONTENTS

	PAGE
THE PARROT'S LANGUAGE	89
THE PRINCE AND HIS SISTER	92
THE CUP OF TEARS	105
TWO LITTLE BOOTS	114
OUR ORPHAN	138
A HERO'S STATUE	144

PROLOGUE

Like unto wheat is truth in this world sown,
And from each grain do many fancies spring;
Happy is he when these to sheaves are grown,
Gath'ring the corn—who forth the chaff doth fling.
Then comes repayment to reward his pains:
Mid storied fancies hid who finds that truth remains.

A GRANDFATHER'S STORY

N old grandfather was leaning back in a large arm-chair, whilst his grandchildren, three fair-haired little ones, were sitting round him to listen to the tale which he told them every evening after supper when they were good.

They were anxiously expectant of a story in reward for exemplary conduct on their side, so the kind grandfather, after coughing to clear his throat, took a pinch of snuff, some grains of which he carefully wiped off with his spotted handkerchief, and, whilst his fingers played with his watch chain, spoke as follows :—

I cannot tell how it came about, but one day, when I was very young, I lost myself on the hills and could not retrace my path, but found myself suddenly in a desert place which was very wild looking and utterly unknown to me. Right and left I saw huge crags; downwards there seemed to be an almost interminable way, whilst upwards there extended an equally interminable but very steep ascent. Down, far down, where the pathway seemed to end, I was just able to see a garden full of flowers; and the wind, when it blew thence, bore with it the most beautiful of perfumes and the warbling of birds. On the other side, on the heights of the hill, on the contrary, there was nothing visible but rocks and the bare earth. No song of birds was borne to me from those peaks, except indeed the screaming of storks, who were flying high above, and no sweet odours were wafted from that desolate place.

I stood still in great uncertainty as to what I should do. How I came to be there at all I could not tell, neither did I seem to remember whence I had come; but whither should I now go? Right and left, as I said before, there were precipices; before me was the difficult rugged pass leading upwards, behind me was the downward slope. I preferred the look of the downward slope, and turning to go by it I heard the sound of voices, when, moving my head in the direction whence it came, I saw on that part of the hill a large number of people who were also going the same way. As they came nearer I saw that they were composed of every class—men and women, young and old, well clad and ill clad, were all mixed up together.

A young woman in many-coloured garments was going in front, leading the way. They all followed her closely, and behaved themselves more like idiots than otherwise, for they kept shouting and holding out their hands in the strangest fashion. I soon saw the reason for that. She had a basket on her arm, and she kept throwing out of it on each side as she went along all kinds of gewgaws and trifles.

Every time she scattered these things abroad there arose bursts of laughter and singing from the one side, or groans and curses from the other. Every one rushed to seize whatever he could lay his hands on. Some of them could only get their palms filled with knick-knacks, others got nothing at all, whilst some managed to get crowns, which they stuck upon their heads, and a large number of women were actually glittering with diamonds. But the greater part of them got nothing, and looked more like beggars than anything else, with wan faces and bloodshot eyes, and garments all torn and ragged, stretching out their empty hands in despair.

But to me the most dreadful thing

was to see how, when the woman threw some coronet or other bauble right and left of her, the mob rushed like madmen and fought with each other in their endeavours to seize it, and often in their struggles some of them would fall right over the precipice into the abyss below.

I wanted to know who this woman was, and who the fools were who ran after her in that manner, and so I went up to her and addressed her politely: 'Good madam, where does this road lead to?'

She turned, and was then in front of me, when I saw to my utmost surprise that she was blind. Yes, actually blind, and yet a large crowd, of people who had their sight, was actually following her. This was strange, I thought.

'This road,' she answered in the sweetest of voices, 'leads to Happiness. Come with me, and if you like you will soon arrive at it.'

When the rest heard her speak

kindly to me, they regarded me with fury, as if they were all envious because she addressed me. For a moment I remained irresolute, when she again said: 'Come with me.'

She spoke in so charming a tone that I answered immediately with some fervour: 'I should like to go, but I am so tired now from my journey.'

'Is that all? Look here; take this gold stick to rest upon when you are fatigued.'

Saying this, she put her hand in her basket and drew out a stick all of gold. No sooner, however, had she held it out to give it me than she by mistake gave it to some one else, who snatched at it and ran away.

I was just going to tell her of her error when a bony hand was suddenly laid upon my shoulder. I was almost frightened, and turned to see whose it was. I saw a very aged woman, clothed in black, with a sad and sympathetic face, and large blue eyes.

'Stop,' she cried in a tremulous voice.

Then looking angrily at the young woman, she said: 'Thou greedy creature, dost thou seek to get this one also?'

'I wish to have him, of course, but perhaps he'll prefer to go with thee. If he prefers thee, I give him to thee.'

The old woman turned to me: 'Why do you desire to follow her? Do you not see the fate of all who go after her?'

'Yes, I do. Down there, when I get to that beautiful garden of beautiful flowers and singing birds, I shall find happiness.'

'True!' cried the young woman, laughing; 'whilst, if you go with her, you will have a dreadful journey up above—at the end of which all she has to give you will be dry bread and cold water when you are hungry and thirsty, a bed of straw to lie down upon when you get to her poor hut and are tired and weary, and only a wooden staff will you have to aid your ascent. But let him go with thee if he wishes—let him go—let him go.'

I did not know what to do. The countenance of the old woman inspired me with more confidence, but the face of the young woman was so much brighter—so much livelier.. Then that rugged ascent repelled me, whereas the downward way looked so easy. The chief thing, however, that led me to prefer to accompany the latter was the beautiful garden full of flowers and singing birds, which I saw in the far distance.

The old woman regarded me with disquietude, and her eyes filled with tears.

'No, no,' she cried with a voice choked by sobs; 'no, I will not let you destroy yourself. I will save you, whether you will or no.'

Saying this she caught me up in her arms and hugged me to her with as much affection as a mother, whilst the young woman, despairing now of gaining possession of me, turned away, and with a scornful laugh, calling out: 'You fool, you fool!' went on her way down, followed by her mad companions.

Then I said to the old woman: 'How is it that this blind person can lead people who have their sight?'

'Do you not know who she is that wanted you to go with her? She is Fortune.'

'Fortune—Fortune!' I cried angrily, and struggled to escape from her hands. 'As long as I have lived I have been trying to find her, and now that I have just succeeded in meeting with her you have made me lose her. Who are you, pray?'

'I am Patience, my child.'

'And what old worn-out gifts have you to bestow on me? If I had gone with her, I should have found happiness.' And I pointed to the charming garden of birds and flowers.

The old woman shook her head, and a bitter smile played upon her lips.

'My child, the truth is that I have no lying gifts to scatter, as Fortune does in her blindness; neither will I promise happiness to every one who asks for it in order to persuade them to follow me. The fact is, that in order to reach the top of the hill you will have to labour hard, and you will be very tired. When you do succeed in reaching it you will not find gardens and flowers and birds. I shall take you to my humble hut, and shall lay down a skin for you to sleep upon, but your sleep will be very sweet, because of your fatigue. When you are rested you will find upon those heights land which you must cultivate with your own hands, and the gardens which you will be able to make will be fairer far than those down there which you so much desire to go to. Ah! if you could but see that garden as it really is.'

'I have seen it,' I said pettishly,

'and there cannot possibly be one more beautiful.'

'Still so confident! Look now and see if it is so fair,' and the old woman took from her breast her own glasses and gave them to me.

I put them to my eyes, when every thing afar off became larger and nearer. I sought for the lovely garden, but I had no sooner turned my glance in that direction than I screamed out, quite frightened at beholding nothing but graves and crosses.

I knelt down before that old woman, Patience, and kissed those wrinkled hands which had kept me from following blind Fortune.

She raised me up with great sweetness: 'Come, let us go on our way, before the night cometh upon our road. Life's day is not long.'

The ascent, as it lay before me, seemed to have no end, but I took courage and began quietly to climb it, and I tried hard to reach the top; but my knees were trembling—they seemed to give under me. 'Ah!' I said, 'if I could only reach the top before nightfall.'

The grandfather suddenly stopped his recital in order to take another pinch of snuff, whilst his grandchildren looked at him with great impatience manifested in their eyes, longing for the end of the tale.

At last the youngest of all, a little girl of six years old, could wait no longer: 'Grandfather, grandfather, did you ever get to the top of that hill?'

The grandfather stroked her fair hair with his hand, and caressed her as he said in an agitated voice: 'My little darling, if I had not got up there I should never have been thy grandfather, and I could not have told thee this story to-day.'

THE MAIDEN'S THREE GIFTS

 POOR woman gave birth to a daughter. Her husband had died a few days before the babe was born, so that she was alone in the world and quite desolate. All her love, therefore, centred upon this child, and, clad as she was in widow's weeds, she clasped it fondly in her arms.

On the third day after its birth three fairies, who greatly commiserated her, came to visit her, and seeing how beautiful the infant was, and how much the mother loved it, they promised it three good gifts.

The first fairy, touching it with her

golden wand, said: 'The day that she is twelve years old a rose shall fall from her mouth every time she laughs.'

The second fairy then touched it with her golden wand: 'The day that she is twelve years old,' she said, 'every time she weeps, pearls shall fall from her eyes.'

And lastly, the third fairy—with her golden wand—also touched her, saying: 'Before your eighteenth year has passed, a prince shall marry you, and you shall become a princess.'

The mother listened to all these promises, and her heart rejoiced exceedingly. She was very, very poor, but she brought up her daughter as well as she could until she was twelve years of age. The evening of the day on which she had completed her twelfth year, the girl laughed right out with joy at something which her mother had said, and immediately the first rose fell from her lips, and when the mother saw it, she remembered all that the fairies had promised, and her motherly heart rejoiced, for she said: 'If one promise be fulfilled, the others will surely follow in their turn.'

The girl was graceful, beautiful, and blithe, and the roses fell from her mouth like rain. The mother, without having the trouble to gather roses, put them all into a basket, and took them to the town and sold them. With the money thus obtained she and the daughter lived—frugally certainly, but nevertheless more comfortably than heretofore. So time went on.

It was winter, and the Queen was going to give a great ball at the palace. She had a beautiful gown, and it was rose colour, so she wanted to have real roses on her head and at her breast to wear with it. She therefore ordered the royal gardener to bring her some; but he said that so much snow had fallen that all the roses were spoilt, and that he could not find even one. The Queen was very angry at this, and told him straightway that she did not believe him, but that he preferred to leave them to perish in the royal garden, adding that she should go and seek for herself another gardener, and dismiss him forthwith.

The poor gardener sighed upon hearing this, and went to look at every garden far and near to see if he could possibly find any roses; but he found none. In the course of his wanderings he happened to pass by the cottage in which dwelt the poor woman and her daughter.

The gardener was so bewildered by his anxiety that he did not look to see where he was going, and never observing a stone that was lying before the cottage, he stumbled over it and fell down. There was something comical in the way in which he fell, for he did not hurt himself, but his fez rolled off his head into the mud and got dirtied.

The girl, who was looking out of the window, could not help laughing when she saw the gardener fall, and down dropped a rose from her mouth and fell into the road right in front of the gardener. When she saw what had occurred she felt a little bit ashamed, and drew back to hide herself, but the gardener, as soon as he saw it, never stayed to pick up his fez but ran quickly to seize the rose. He could not believe his own eyes. How did it come there? Perhaps it was done by magic. Anyhow, it was a real and beautiful rose, and smelt better than those of April. But one rose was of no use for the Queen. He must have ten, and where could he find the others?

Since, however, it had fallen just in front of that house, the people who lived there might know something about it. 'Anyhow, I'll knock,' he said to himself.

So without any more ado he knocked at the door, which the mother immediately opened. 'Well, my good man, what do you want?' she asked.

And then he told her all about the Queen and the ball, and how he had suddenly found a rose outside her house, when he was almost in a state of despair. After the mother heard all this, she said: 'Take this one then, and go to the Queen, and tell her that there is only one rose-tree which is able to produce such roses, and that on the day of the ball I will cut some, and take her as many as she desires.'

The gardener immediately went to the Queen with the one rose, and told her what the woman had said, whereat the Queen was greatly overjoyed. She put the rose into her bosom, and it filled the whole palace with its scent.

When the day of the ball arrived, the Queen ordered the gardener to fetch both the woman and the roses, and about noon the mother arrived at the palace, bringing with her a covered basket, and after she had saluted her

Majesty, she uncovered it and presented the roses to her.

No sooner had the Queen seen them than she was so delighted that she embraced and kissed the poor woman warmly. There were ten dozen in the basket, and what roses! each was more beautiful than the other.

'Madam,' said the Queen, 'I have a favour to ask of you. Sell me the rose-tree which bears these roses. I will give you whatever you may demand for it.'

But the mother answered: 'Much honoured Queen, I cannot do this with my rose-tree. I cannot sell it. Only one thing can I do, if you are willing. You have a Prince, and I will bestow it on the Prince, to have it for his own, and to keep it honoured and loved as if it were a living princess.'

'Your wish shall be granted, madam, so that we may only have the rose-tree in the palace; and you may come with it, and live near us also.'

'I have no wish for that, your Majesty. My rose-tree is the only thing I care for. I wish that to be happy, for it is all that I have to love in the world. I believe all your words, but still the world is the world. Swear to me, by the life of your son, that it shall be as you say.'

'I swear to you, by the life of my only son, that the tree which brings forth these roses shall be honoured in this palace as if it were a real living princess.'

'May God grant you a long life, my Queen. Come by yourself to-morrow, and take away the rose-tree from my house.'

The ball took place in the palace that evening, and all wondered at the Queen's roses. Where had she found them? It was quite a marvel. Such flowers in the middle of winter!

The next morning the Queen lost

no time before going to secure the rose-tree. When the Prince heard of the agreement which his mother had made with the woman, he jumped for joy, and got a golden vase ready in the palace in which the rose-tree was to be planted. The Queen and Prince went together in a gold chariot, and stopping before the humble cottage where the mother and daughter dwelt, they alighted. The mother had mentioned nothing to her daughter, except that the Queen kindly intended to come in person to thank her for the gift of roses.

As soon as the mother and daughter went out to receive the royal visitors, the daughter, as she bent down to kiss the Queen's hand, smiled merely from a grateful feeling, and a rose fell from her mouth. The Queen at first did not understand how this came to pass; but the Prince ran immediately to pick it up to give to his mother, and the girl, beholding him, smiled again in her great joy, when the second rose fell.

At one and the same moment the Queen and the Prince understood it all. The Queen became very angry, because she remembered directly that she was bound by her oath to receive the girl as a daughter-in-law. She turned, however, to look at her again, when she saw that the girl was really so very beautiful and so very good, that without a moment's longer reserve she threw her arms around her, saying aloud as she kissed her: 'You are a poor girl no longer, but a princess henceforth. You shall come and live in our palace—you and your good mother also.'

'Now that it has all turned out exactly as you wished it,' she added, addressing the mother, 'tell me, lady co-mother-in-law, how your daughter acquired so great a charm as to shower roses from her mouth whenever she laughs.'

The mother immediately told her all about the fairies and their three promised gifts to her daughter when she was an infant, and how the first and the last promise had both come true.

'The second has not taken place then,' said the Queen with some curiosity. 'How was it that did not happen? for, poor as you were, had pearls fallen from her eyes you could have sold them.'

'That did not happen,' answered the mother, 'because I never made her weep; I sought only to see her happy and smiling, preferring to live poor in my daughter's gladness than to become rich by her grief.'

When the Queen heard these words she embraced and kissed her, saying: 'You have indeed been a good mother, and it is an honour to a Queen to make you her co-mother-in-law.'

The girl, who had listened to all that her mother had said, was now so overcome by her emotion that her eyes filled with tears, and two large pearls rolled down. The Prince stooped to pick them up.

'These are not tears of sorrow,' he said; 'they are tears of joy. I will take them and have them made into earrings, and you shall wear them on the day on which you become my princess.'

THE MUSICIAN AND THE DANCER

OWN yonder by the threshing-floors, where the husbandmen thresh out their corn, some large ants as black as negroes once established themselves and built their nests. They settled themselves in that place in order to be near good and wholesome food, such as wheat, barley, and maize, which they carried off, whether the farmers liked it or no.

These ants prospered and became so numerous that they formed themselves into a kingdom, and had their own king.

The King, who was an old ant, was

very wise and courageous. As he was a real king he wore a golden crown upon his head, and held a golden sceptre in his hand.

His crown was a small piece of round gold wire, and fitted his head splendidly. His soldiers in one of their raids had found it in a country-maiden's casket, when they took possession of it, and presented it to their sovereign. In the same way they came across the sceptre, which they saw one day on the threshing-floor, and appropriated in like manner. It was nothing more than a little gold watch-key, which had dropped off the chain of the village steward, but that was of no consequence, because as soon as the royal hand grasped it, it derived value from that circumstance alone.

The King had his own carriage. It was made out of a nut-shell, and was drawn by two swift and well-harnessed beetles, who, like all royal horses, were well trained. The King generally drove out, because his Majesty was now so aged that he had become quite white.

So you see that he had every blessing, and his people loved him very much. But he was not happy, he was weary and satiated, and no longer found pleasure in anything.

One day there was a great tumult in the ant kingdom. A regiment of soldiers, which had gone out upon an excursion, returned after a brilliant victory, and brought back great spoils, and also four prisoners.

The King, from the balcony of his palace, with his crown on his head and his sceptre in his hand, greeted his army as it marched before him in great order, saluting him with, 'Long live the King.' Then he ordered that the four prisoners should be brought before him, in order that he might determine what should be done with them.

The first captive was a spider.

'What is your name?' asked the King.

'Spider,' she answered humbly, and did homage with her two forelegs.

'Where were you born?' said the King.

'I was born in the mill's dark cellar.'

After many other questions the King again said: 'What art do you know?'

'I know how to weave,' said the spider. 'No one can surpass me in weaving. I am the best weaver in the world.'

'Good,' said the King; 'you shall weave me some cloth for my palace, and if your work is satisfactory, I will set you free; if not, I shall hand you over to my soldiers to be cut in pieces. Shut her up in prison and let her begin at once.'

As the King decreed this he lowered his sceptre and struck it on the ground, when immediately a detachment of ten soldiers dragged off the spider by her feet, and confined her in a cell.

The second prisoner, which was a bee, was then brought forward. The King in like manner questioned her. She said her name was 'Bee,' and did him obeisance. Upon his inquiring where she was born, she replied: 'In a hive, which was a house built for a number of bees to live in.'

'Do you know any trade or profession?' inquired the King.

'Certainly, your Majesty, I know how to make a most delicious food. No one can excel me.'

'Good!' said the King. 'You shall make all the sweetmeats which I shall require at a forthcoming festival, when the peasants spread their threshing-floors, and then, if I am pleased with them, I will release you; but if not, I shall order my soldiers to cut off your head. Confine her, and let her begin at once.'

Again he knocked with his sceptre, and the detachment of soldiers led the bee off to prison, when the King said:

'Bring in the two other prisoners together, that we may finish with them, as I have other business of the kingdom on hand.'

Then were brought in together the third and fourth captives. The third was a grasshopper, and the fourth a cricket.

When they were asked the customary questions as to their places of birth, the first replied: 'At the roots of a bush of thyme.' And the other: 'In the air.' When the King proceeded with: 'And what arts do you know?'

'I know how to sing,' cried the cricket.

'And I how to dance,' said the grasshopper.

'Splendid arts, truly, both the one and the other,' called out the King in a rage, and he knocked with his sceptre so loudly that he frightened all his courtiers and soldiers, as well as the two prisoners. 'Since you know nothing, you are plainly of no use.

I shall have you cut up, the pair of you.'

'Please, your Majesty,' said the cricket boldly, whilst the grasshopper trembled with fear: 'Can we do nothing? do we know nothing? because this lady and myself cannot weave like the spider or make sweetmeats like the bee? We are worthy people, and the whole world loves us. We amuse all the insects on both hill and plain; we make life in the long summer days when the sun is hot a little less wearisome; then I sing, and she dances, and for those who see and hear us time soon passes. Allow us the same privilege before your Majesty, and you can then judge if we be deserving of freedom or death.'

The King was not hard-hearted, and after hearing this plea of the cricket, he said: 'I grant your request. I have small time to divert myself, and if you can succeed in giving me a little pleasure in a short space of time, I will give you both your liberty, and grant you each any favour which you may ask.'

He gave orders to release them. The cricket then began to sing with all the skill which she possessed, and the grasshopper danced at the same time. Neither the King nor his courtiers or soldiers had ever heard so sweet a voice, nor seen so artistic a dance. His Majesty was hugely delighted; his old face laughed all over, and he struck with his sceptre out of very joy, and shouted: 'Well done! Bravo! I'll free you—I'll free you. I only request that whenever you have the time or the inclination, that you will come and amuse myself and subjects a little. Labour is good, but life wants some few pleasures also. I told you that I would grant you any favour which you asked for. Ask now what you will.'

Then the cricket said pleadingly,

'Your Majesty, I ask this favour—that the poor spider may be released.'

'You have a good heart,' answered the King; 'be it so.' And he turned to the grasshopper: 'And what favour do you ask, madam dancer?'

'May it please your Majesty to release the bee?'

'And you too have a good heart—your wish is granted.' And the King ordered the release of the prisoners.

They were immediately set free, and all the ants conducted them out of the ant-hills, when the cricket, full of joy, sang along the road—

> 'Zi zi zi and zi zi zi,
> May our Lord the King live joyfully,
> And all his people as well as he.'

THE COUSIN OF THE ROSE

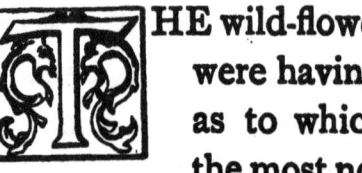HE wild-flowers of the fields were having a great debate as to which of them was the most noble. Each said so of itself, and in support of its claims brought either the varied colours of its blossoms, or the dewy freshness of its leaves, or its sweet scent. All of a sudden the Thistle appeared in their midst.

They looked at her with astonishment. What could she have to say for herself? Could she boast of any worth? Why did she not stoop and look at herself in the water?

The Thistle, however, never heeded their contemptuous remarks, but began vociferating as loudly as she could, shaking her thorny leaves all the while: 'Ha, ha! who dares to talk here about nobility? Is it you, Mistress Thyme, who lights the village ovens; or you, Lady Marjorum, whom the cook makes use of for her dishes; or perhaps 'tis old Dame Mallow, whom the apothecaries employ to make a lenitive; or Camomile, with his yellow buds! No one here except myself has any right to talk about nobility.'

All the wild-flowers, when they heard these words, were amazed at the insolence of the Thistle. Many laughed outright, and others were very angry, but they hardly dared to show what they felt, because they were afraid of the Thistle's thorns.

But the Thistle, in no wise abashed, cried out louder than ever: 'It seems a strange thing to me that you doubt my worth, or make a pretence of so doing. Anyhow, I will explain to you how it is. Which now, in the whole world, is considered the noblest flower?'

All cried out at once: 'The Rose, the Rose!'

'Well, then, I am the cousin of the Rose.'

At this assertion of the Thistle all the wild-flowers began to shout more than ever; they had expected something else—certainly not this.

Mother Thyme, who had noted what the Thistle had said about herself, cried out in a rage: 'You—cousin to the Rose! How is that, pray?'

'I will show you in a minute.'

'You will show us, will you?' cried Marjorum, who had plucked up a little courage.

'Since you are the Rose's cousin, you ought to resemble her,' said the Camomile, who had become as white as a sheet on account of the rudeness of the Thistle.

'Certainly, I resemble her.'

All the wild-flowers started up

from their roots to see how she could resemble the Rose, and even the Cyclamen came out of her hole in the rock.

'Where are your beautiful roses?' cried the Thyme.

'Oh, I haven't got any roses!' answered the Thistle somewhat humbly.

'Where is your lovely scent?' cried Marjorum.

'I haven't got any scent,' answered the Thistle still more humbly.

'Then what have you got that you resemble your cousin in?' cried out five wild-flowers all together, almost choked by their impatience.

'I have got thorns, and thus I resemble my cousin the Rose.'

Then there came forth quite a storm of jeers and hisses, shouts and laughter.

'See here now,' cried all the wild-flowers, 'much joy may you have with this your resemblance. You won't find that any one will put on one side the many perfections of the Rose to find some resemblance with you in her one defect.'

The Thistle, now thoroughly ashamed, went to hide herself in a trench, and her thorns grew larger because of her rage. Nevertheless, whenever she looked at herself, she admired herself more and more, and still thought that she resembled her cousin the Rose.

THE DEATH OF THE POPPY

T was the time of beautiful spring—the sky above was a clear blue, and the meadows beneath were a vivid green. In one corner of a small field, which the wheat that was sown there had left untouched, a wild violet was growing. The violet was in flower; she had two blossoms like two blue eyes, and looked about her to see what was going on in her neighbourhood, but her blooms were half closed as a strong light oppressed her.

A little way off, right in the midst of the green corn, a tall poppy flaunted herself. As it was Sunday she wore her green gown and her crimson cap, and she thought that she was indeed somebody, and that there was no one else like her.

The Violet saw her and said to herself: 'How pretty, but how fantastic!'

The Poppy also, who just deigned a glance at the violet from a corner of her eye, said: 'Pretty, but how mean!'

Neither one told the other what it thought, and the Poppy after a little while said in a somewhat contempuous manner: 'Good morning, neighbour.'

'Good morning,' replied the Violet dryly.

'I see you have got on your working-day gown. Did not the dressmaker finish your new one?' This the Poppy said on purpose to tease her.

'I did not order a gown, neither do I care how I am dressed; fancy colours do not suit me; I am quite content with what I have; I possess a perfume,' replied the Violet.

'Well and good—every one has his own ideas; for myself I like to be well dressed. How do you like my gown and cap?'

'Very beautiful; you make a grand show.'

'You can't see me so well at that distance. Why don't you come nearer? I can't understand your fancy for always sitting outside of the field, away from us. To be sure, as you have not got fine clothes, it does not matter. However, I am not proud.'

As the Poppy said this she tossed her head with its red cap from right to left.

The Violet was angry at this, and answered: 'As you are not in your own home, it is absurd for you to make any invitations. Where you have enthroned yourself and are displaying your charms is not your proper place; it belongs to the wheat. I am here alone, and a rustic, but the spot is my own, and I am satisfied.'

When she had said this she turned away her blue eyes to the other side, and looked at a white butterfly who was fluttering and spreading out her wings in the sunshine.

The Poppy bit her lips and made no reply. After a little while she also turned round, and said to a pale Anemone who was near her: 'A good many people, if they are insolent, at least they know their place, and don't come and intrude upon their betters.'

It was not very long before the farmer, who had sown the field with wheat, came to see how it was getting on. He never noticed the pale Anemone, but trod upon her with his heavy foot and crushed her, but when he saw the crimson-capped Poppy afar off, he shouted: 'You weed, what do you here, spoiling my wheat?'

And he stretched out his big fingers, and seizing her pulled her up and threw her away near the Violet. Then he stood still, and looking all about with a pleased expression, said: 'What a lovely perfume there is here; it must be a violet in blossom. Ha! here it is.' And he passed on his way without touching it, and was careful not to tread upon it.

The Poppy lay where she had fallen,—her green gown was soiled with dirt, her red cap was torn and ragged. At eventide she expired. A Thistle then turned, and said to the Violet: 'It served her right. Why did she come and fix herself where she was not planted?'

'It is sinful to accuse her now,' answered the Violet in a sad voice. And she bent down sorrowfully as two tears like two glistening dewdrops fell from her blue eyes.

THE WINGS OF THE SOUL

POOR little orphan! She never knew her mother, who died a few days after she was born, and she lost her father when she was only three years old. He was but a poor workingman, and when he died suddenly only two sixpences and one pennypiece were found in his drawers. He had no relations, but the neighbours made a collection in order to bury him, and a charitable lady succeeded in getting his bereaved child into an orphanage.

This little orphan was pale and pensive. She never smiled, nor had any desire to play with the other orphans. But if she were not cheerful she was at least good, and was beloved by every one in the orphanage. When she was eight years of age she was seized with a serious illness, and the doctors, despairing of her life, lamented her as one already dead. Nevertheless, she lived on and recovered, but this recovery was a doubtful benefit, for her illness left behind it that for which there was no cure. She had lost all power in both feet, and could no longer use them, nor walk about.

From morning till night she had to sit in a large easy-chair, whilst all the other orphans were running and jumping about in the courtyard and garden belonging to the orphanage, and when she turned her thoughtful, sad little face to look at them, tears would fall from her eyes.

She would often gaze down at those small shoes of hers, which were always untrodden, always new, and never dusty; and then she would look at those of the other children that were dirty and worn by running about the stony roads. Ah, how she envied them! She thought that if she could but use her feet she would never care to sit quiet again; she would run and spring, jump about, climb trees, and be up to all kinds of mischief, even if she should get punished by her teachers. What would any punishment be in comparison with this perpetual affliction!

Always sitting in an easy-chair, she was sometimes carried into the garden and placed in a shady spot, or else, if the weather was bad, she sat by the window, so that she could look out. They all, however, sympathised with her, and would often go and sit by her side and try to amuse her, so that she might forget her misfortune, but they could not succeed. The child would thank them with a sad smile for so much goodness on their part, but she would turn away her sorrowful little head.

Her only consolation was at night, when she lay in her little bed. Then, whilst the light flickered from a hanging lamp, she would fix her eyes upon the opposite wall, where there was a large and beautiful picture.

The painter had himself given this picture to the orphanage, and it represented a winged angel, who was flying to heaven, holding in his hands another very small angel, who did not seem able to fly by himself, because he was so very small. The little orphan looked at this picture so often with the eyes of her mind, that in a short time it seemed to her that the lifeless colours became animated, and that the angel was no longer a painted one, but a true living angel, and that it was her very self that he was holding by the hand and guiding.

Thus, whilst her body was stretched upon her bed, her spirit went along with the angel. If her body had no feet to walk with, her soul had wings and could fly. And when she would at last close her eyes from very weariness, it seemed to her as if she had only returned from taking a long journey with the angel, and two or three times she fancied that the angel kissed her sleeping eyes, and one night she thought that he said softly, whilst she slept: 'Why wish for feet when you have wings?'

Upon a winter's day, when the snow was falling, and it was very cold, the little orphan was so weak that the directress had removed her into a room where there was a fire.

As they were conversing, the child said: 'Did I never have a mother?'

'How could you not have one?' answered the directress.

'Then, where is she? How is it that I have never seen her?'

'Because you were so very young when she was taken.'

'Taken where?'

'Up on high—to a far-off—far-off place.' And she pointed to heaven.

'Why does she never come to see me?' said the orphan sorrowfully.

'Because they who go up there never return.'

'Ah, how I wish that I could go and see her and talk to her!—yes, talk to her. You are so very, very kind, can you not send me there?' she asked in an anxious tone.

'No one can go thither of his own free will, my dear little girl. It is very far—very high. They are not feet that are needed; one must have wings for that.'

The orphan said no more, a smile suddenly lighted up her sad little face and brightened her pale lips, and she laughed. That evening, as she was more tired and weaker than usual, she went early to bed. As on former nights the angel came again to take her out, and for the first time she had the courage to speak to him. 'I do so long to go and see my mother,' she whispered. 'Could not you who are so good take me to her?'

'It is a long way—you would be tired,' he answered.

'I should not be tired, because I should be going to find my mother.'

'Do you know that every one who goeth there can never return?'

'Why should I wish to return, when I should be with my mother?'

'Your wish shall be fulfilled,' said the angel with emotion. 'Let us go, and then you will find your mother.'

And he stretched out his hands and took her in his arms.

Early in the morning they found her lying lifeless on her little bed. All wept; her face alone seemed to be smiling with joy, for she had gone to find her mother.

THE CUCKOO CLOCK

 A CLOCK hung on the wall of a dining-room. This clock, however, did not follow the usual custom of clocks. It did not strike the hours—oh dear, no! A little door above its face would open instead, and out would come a cuckoo, which flapped its wings and called out, 'Cuckoo! Cuckoo!' It called this out as many times as the strokes of the hour. Then it went back again, and the door shut after it.

The black cat of the house beheld this bird with great longing, and every time he heard it he reared himself up below and mewed terribly. As he looked at it with flaming eyes, he said to himself: 'If I could get that bird in my claws, what a nice tender bit it would be. 'Tis worth all the mice which I have to run about the cellar to catch.'

But the clock was hanging high, and he could find no way to get up to it. This difficulty increased his desire to get it. Cats, like men, always desire the most that which they are not able to obtain.

The longing after this bird got so great a hold upon him that he no longer cared for mice, and whilst they disported themselves in the cellar, the cat, instead of hunting them, sat hour after hour hungry in front of the clock, waiting for the cuckoo. At last he got quite weak for want of food, and became almost a skeleton.

By evil chance the maid one day brought in a ladder in order to dust the pictures and also the clock. The cat watched till she went out of the room, and as she left the ladder near the clock, he lost no time, but ran up it directly. It happened to be just ten o'clock, so the little door opened, and out came the cuckoo, who was going to call out 'Cuckoo' ten times, but it had only got as far as five when the cat suddenly dashed at it with his claws—which certainly stopped its voice, but at the same time down fell the clock off the nail with a great noise to the ground, and lay there shattered. The cat fled. He knew that he had done mischief and that he would be beaten; so he ran and hid himself under the sofa, but the maid found him and gave him a good round of forty stripes or more.

On account of the fall the works of the clock were quite spoilt, and the little cuckoo remained outside on the floor, with its wings spread out, as if it had been killed.

All the time the cat was being beaten he said to himself: 'I'm getting the stick now, but soon I'll be getting the little bird. How delicate its flesh will be! It will be quite worth all the pain this stick is giving me.' And then, whilst even the maid was running after him to drive him out of the house, he managed very cleverly as he got away to snatch up the bird with his teeth, and run with it down into the dark cellar, in order to eat it in peace.

And then he found out his folly. After all his trouble and watching, his fasting and the beating which the maid had given him, this precious bird, which he fancied must be more delicate than a new-born mouseling, and more wholesome than fish-bones, could not be eaten—it was only wood, only wood.

THE ROOK'S BATH

 ROOK who, from a tree in a wood, could look down upon some pigeons in a pigeonry, became quite envious of the good life they led, and wished that she could live in a pigeonry.

A Cuckoo, hearing her sighing and complaining spoke to her, saying: 'What's the matter, cousin?'

'What's the matter? I mourn my fate in not being a pigeon and well taken care of. Look there.' And she lifted up one leg and pointed to the pigeons, who were in the yard picking up heaps of corn.

'And that makes you envious, poor

thing? Well, it's easy enough to alter it.'

'How?' cried the Rook eagerly.

'Don't you see that all those pigeons are quite white? Go and whiten yourself, and feed with them, for they will all welcome you as a pigeon, and you will be well cared for.'

The Rook thanked the Cuckoo, and acted according to her advice. She went to the mill-stream, and bathed in the water, and whilst wet got into the mill through a little window when the miller was away, and rolling herself in the flour made herself as white as the pigeons. Thus changed, she flew to a branch of a tree near the river, and looked at herself in the water, when she actually did not know herself again.

Then she flew to the pigeon-house and mixed with the pigeons. So she was taken for a pigeon and ate well, and did nothing all the day long.

The owner of the pigeons had company coming one day, and wished therefore to kill some pigeons. He picked out several, and among them the Rook. As soon as she saw the knife made ready to kill her, she almost lost her wits from sheer fright and shrieked out, K-r-a—K-r-a.

When the owner saw that she was no pigeon he did not kill her, but in order to punish her he cut off her wings and tail, and drove her out of the pigeonry.

It was early in the morning. Suddenly out from among the trees the Cuckoo called out: 'Cuckoo—cuckoo.'

The Rook turned round angrily, and cried: 'You gave me very fine advice!'

But the Cuckoo made no other answer than by calling out jeeringly: 'Cuckoo—cuckoo.'

Then the Rook became more angry than before, and tried to fly at her to pick out her eyes, but she could not fly, and was beside herself with rage.

A plant of garlic which happened to be growing near then sang out—

> 'Greedy and silly art thou,
> Speak not of it again;
> But leave your anger and laugh,
> Thou art saved with little pain,
> Thou art saved with little pain.
>
> 'Put into thy empty head
> Some sense and wisdom too,
> And never follow more
> What a cuckoo bids thee do,
> What a cuckoo bids thee do.'

THE MOTHER'S BLESSING

ONCE upon a time there was a merchant, and he had two male children.

For a while everything went on well, but suddenly his affairs seemed to take a turn, and first one speculation went wrong, and then another, till at last he lost nearly all his money. So he said to his sorrowing wife: 'Wife, nothing else is left me to do—I must go on my journeys again, and get some more money, in order that we may have something to bring up our children upon, and have a competence for our old age. I leave you to be the guardian of our children, and may we be happily reunited once more.'

He kissed his weeping wife and children and departed. Before he went he gave his wife all the money he had to supply the necessities of the household until his return; but years went on and the wife became old, and the children grew up, and yet the merchant came not back. The small amount of money which he left had long been spent, but the sons concealed this from the mother, lest it should cause her some anxiety.

They told her that they were at school all day, but they were out at service, and with the pay they received they managed to provide for the house whilst the mother thought that everything was procured with the money which the father had left, and therefore she was quite content.

It came to pass, however, that one day there was not a farthing in the house, and the mother became ill. What was to be done?

Then the younger son said to his elder brother: 'I see no alternative but that you take and sell me for a slave. In this way you will procure money enough to enable our mother to enjoy her life.'

To this the elder brother made answer: 'You say truly; I can see no other way, but you shall not be sold. It had better be myself, because I am taller and stronger, and therefore shall fetch more money. As you are the younger, you shall stay at home, and take care of our mother.'

The younger brother, however, would not agree to this at all, so after a time the elder said: 'Well—let it be so—it shall be as you wish, brother;' and he kissed and embraced him, and then they went together to their mother.

'Mother,' said the elder son, 'one of us ought to go and travel, in order that our father may be found. When he left us we were only little children, but now we are grown up. He may have need of one of us in a foreign land. So the younger of us will go, and the elder will remain with you.'

'Alas!' cried the mother, 'I wished to have you both always with me, but that is not the will of God. As you have said, so let it be. One shall go, and the other shall stay.'

Then the younger son knelt down, and kissed his mother's hand whilst his tears fell fast upon it, for he had no hope ever to see her again. And his mother clasped him in her arms and embraced him tenderly, saying: 'Go in peace, my son, and the blessing of thy mother keep thee from every danger on the road,' and taking a little silver charm off her own neck, she hung it around that of her son.

The two brothers left the house and walked the whole day, the elder leading the younger by a rope bound round him and shouting aloud as he went along: 'Who wants a slave. I have a slave to sell.'

Night was now coming on, and nobody had bought him, so they both began to lose hope, but on a sudden a window high up in a tower was opened, and an old man with a white cap on looked out and cried: 'How much will you sell your slave for?'

'For a sieve of florins.'

'He is very dear, but never mind, I'll buy him. Wait and I'll come down to you.'

The old man Drako came down and unlocked the tower gate with an iron key, and he took his slave, and gave a sieve of florins to his brother for him, who after taking them went back to his mother. He did not however show her the florins but hid them away, and only took out one at a time to spend. He told his mother that he had made haste to return to her after he had seen his brother on board a ship, and had bidden him farewell. This was the first untruth that he had ever told, so he became very red, and his tongue seemed tied, as it were. What could he do, he must seek his mother's welfare, he thought.

This falsehood after all happened to be half the truth, for the old man who had bought his brother took ship the next day for foreign parts, and his slave went with him.

At first the voyage was pleasant enough, and the bark danced along with sails fully spread, whilst the sailors sang, and the old man in his white cap sat at the prow smoking. All were rejoicing, the slave only excepted, and he was sad, bound as he was, with his head to the mast, by the wicked old man his master, who feared that he might try to escape. The slave was suffering, but nevertheless his very pains seemed sweet, when he thought that now his mother could be well cared for.

Suddenly a very black cloud appeared in the distance, and by degrees veiled the whole of the sky and obscured the sun. The sea became dark, and the waves arose and went roaring round the ship, like hungry wild beasts. The captain, sailors, and all ran hither and thither in their fright, whilst the old man was so beside himself with fear that even the white cap upon his head shook. The slave, however, who was tied to the mast, waited the end patiently.

Suddenly a huge fierce wave came speeding on, and turning the vessel over as if it had been a mere walnut shell, cast it upon a rock. The sea was covered in a moment with broken and shattered spars. The men were all lost, the only thing that was left was the old man's white cap, which the waves tossed from one to the other as if in sport.

The slave alone was not drowned. He remained bound as before to a large fragment of the mast, and was borne onwards by the waves; but, tied as he was, he was unable to free his hands. Presently, however, a large fish—a dolphin—swam up close to him. At first he was somewhat alarmed, thinking that it was going to devour him, and he closed his eyes, when the dolphin said: 'Fear nothing. I have come to save you—sent hither by your mother's blessing.' And, biting the cord asunder with his great mouth, he set him free.

'Now, get on my back,' he cried, 'and hold fast. I will take you to dry land, where you will soon find your father.' And, truly, he carried him through the waves as swiftly as though he had been a winged horse, till he came to a rocky peak, and there left him. He was tired, however, and wet, and was unable to walk; but in a little while a great crab came along, and then a second, and then a third, with a large number of other crabs following. He was a little terrified as he heard the grinding of their claws, and again he closed his eyes, for he could not run away. Then the foremost crab plucked him with his claw, and whispered: 'Don't fear anything. We shall not do you any harm—good rather. Your mother's blessing hath sent us.'

All the crabs then took him up by his clothes with their claws, and drawing him along the sands, carried him to a place where there was a cross road, and there left him.

After a short time an old man with snow-white hair, who was a rich merchant, and who was followed by his slaves, came by that way, and seeing him, had pity on him, saying: 'Take this young man home to my house.'

When the poor youth heard these words he opened his eyes: 'God bless you, Master,' he cried, 'for this good deed. I do not wish to die before I see my father and mother.'

The old merchant wept: 'I too had wife and children,' he answered; 'but necessity obliged me to leave them and go away to a foreign land.'

The slaves then took up the young man and carried him into the house. As his clothes were wet and torn, they brought him others to put on, and as he was taking off his own garments the amulet that hung round his neck was seen.

'Halloo! what is that which you are wearing?' cried the merchant.

The youth told the whole story, and as the merchant listened, he trembled, and his face flushed, whilst the tears fell from his eyes. At last he put out his hand and took hold of the amulet, and when he saw it, he embraced and kissed the young man. 'My son—my good son!' he cried, 'thy mother's blessing hath brought thee to thy father's arms.'

On the very next day he manned a large ship, and loaded it with all the wealth which he had accumulated in foreign parts, and taking his son with him, returned home. The day he arrived it so happened that the elder brother had just spent the last florin left in the sieve, and as his mother was still ill, he knew not what to do, when the news was brought to him that his father and brother had both come back together. He was now frantic with joy, by turns dancing, singing, laughing, and weeping. When, after a little while, they reached the house, the poor mother, who was very weak from her long sickness, was unable to rally at seeing her husband again; but when she heard what her son had done for her sake, she embraced each one of the three, and kissing them all round died in great contentment.

THE FOOLISH CRICKET

CRICKET in a plane-tree sang from morning till night. He had the sweetest voice possible, and every one listened to him with delight. A wasp alone was not well pleased, because she had no voice herself, and was jealous. Going towards the Cricket she said: 'Certainly you have a fine voice—no one can equal you in that. If your face and figure were a little better, you would enchant the whole world.'

'What is there in it, madam, that does not please you?' said the Cricket somewhat offended.

'What is there? why, just look at me, and then look at yourself; you will see well enough what an elegant figure I possess—what a delicate waist! what grace and dignity in every motion! You have no waist at all, only a thick ugly stomach. 'Tis a pity with such a voice!'

The Cricket stooped and looked at himself with his great parti-coloured eyes, and he looked at the Wasp also, and he saw that she was right.

'What would you have me do? Nature made me thus,' he answered sorrowfully.

'Then Nature did you a wrong, but you can set it right yourself.'

'How can I set it right?'

'Do not eat or drink anything for a few days, and you'll see what will come of it. You will then have a beautiful voice, and a beautiful shape as well, nothing will be wanting.'

The Wasp flew away, and the Cricket was left considering; he determined, however, to put the kind advice of the Wasp into practice, and neither ate or drank anything all that day, nor on the day following. Both hunger and thirst assailed him, but he had patience. The Wasp, as she flew past, saw him and cried out: 'Very good! how different from yesterday. You see what has come from my advice. In two or three days you will have a waist like mine.'

The Cricket believed her, and put nothing into his mouth. By the evening, however, he had lost his voice from sheer weakness, and the next morning he died.

The Wasp passed by, and seeing him lying there dead she merely said jeeringly: 'You are very beautiful now, to be sure, you silly creature!'

THE TWO SNAILS

OWN in our garden among the fallen leaves there are two kinds of snails. Some walk about always carrying their houses on their backs, and others have no houses at all to carry. How all this came about was explained to me by an old lizard, who also lives in our garden, and who knows every legend in the whole world.

Once upon a time there was an old snail who had two children. He was not at the trouble of carrying his house. Oh no; but he had a nice little stone house in which he lived, and when he wished to browse upon the green herbs, he went out, and returned to it when he chose. The ants had built this little house, for they are very good builders, and it was certainly very comfortable, for the door shut well, and although the roof was rather low, it did not leak. When his two children grew up, as they could no longer live all together in the same house, he resolved to have one similar to his own built for each of them, and made an agreement with the ants to build two such, for the payment of two hundred grains of wheat and one hundred grains of barley, all of which he had carefully stored up.

The children lived very comfortably in their houses when they were built, but they did not love their father as they ought, or showed any gratitude for what he had done, but on the contrary they disobeyed and often vexed him. The worst of all was, that being now old, and not able to go out in the damp after rain, because he was subject to rheumatism, his children left him alone, and took no care of him, quite forgetting how he had cared for them when they were little. They fed well, for their chief fault was greediness; but they never brought him a fresh young leaf, or a tender flower to nibble. On account of this and many other things he got so angry one evening that he took up a piece of straw, with the intention of beating them, as they did not attend to his words. They managed, however, to escape this punishment, for one ran right away out of his house, and the other curled himself up at the end of his, so the old snail, being inflamed with rage, cursed them both, saying: 'You who have hid yourself in your house shall never leave it again, but shall always have to carry it on your back wherever you go; and you, who have fled from yours, shall never have another to live in at all.' And with all the strength which he had he threw the empty house of the one into a pool of water, adding : 'My last curse is that because of your greediness water shall always dribble from your mouths, and soil every place where you go.'

Because of his great grief, however, the poor old snail was soon after seized with a fit of apoplexy, and died. But it seems that his curse was fulfilled upon his children and children's children, and all their descendants, down to the present time. All this was told me by the old lizard in our garden, and so I tell it to you.

THE ENCHANTED FOUNTAIN.

THE ENCHANTED FOUNTAIN

PHASOULAKI was an extremely small child. When he was born they said he was no larger than a kidney bean, and so they called him Phasoulaki = little kidney bean.

His father had a flock of sheep, which he took to browse in the meadows. One day, as he wanted to go into the country, he called Phasoulaki to him and said: 'Phasoulaki, dost thou think thou'rt able to go with the sheep to-day?'

'Why shouldn't I be able, father? Send me, and thou'lt soon see.'

Then the father said: 'Thou must

be very careful of this. There are three large plantain trees down there, and near them is a fountain which is enclosed with marble; if thou'rt ever so thirsty thou must not open it to drink the water, because that fountain is enchanted.'

'All right, father,' said Phasoulaki.

So he took the sheep and led them away to browse, and about noon he guided them to a place where some large plantains were growing, near to which he knew there was a spring of water where they would be able to drink, and himself also, for he too was very thirsty. When he reached the spot he found that the trench was quite dry. What was he to do? There was no other water visible, and he felt much distressed at this misfortune, for his sheep were parched and bleating, and were even licking the stones.

Phasoulaki turned away and went in another direction until he came where three plantains much larger than any of the others were growing, so tall were they that they almost touched the skies, and down by their roots he saw a round marble slab covering the top of a fountain. High above the marble there was a silver cup hanging, fastened by three chains to three branches of the three trees.

Phasoulaki stood there a very long while, not knowing what to do. If he did not give the sheep any water they would all die, and in that case how could he go back to his father in the evening? And he himself had so great a thirst that his tongue lolled out, just as if it belonged to the mouth of a dog. But then again how could he disobey his father who had told him not to go near that fountain.

Whilst he was in this perplexity he saw a little bird with golden wings fly down and perch upon the hanging cup, skipping about and fluttering round its rim, and it sang in a human voice—

'Oh, the fountain's water is sweet,
   And the running water is clear,
Happy is he who to drink it is meet,
   Luckless the wight who fleeth for fear.'

Phasoulaki did not hesitate any longer, but stooped down to open the marble lid. But he could not move it, for it was as large and heavy as a millstone. Whilst he was vainly endeavouring to open it he saw a small gold padlock at one corner of the marble, but there was no key with it. Then the bird sang again—

'The poor little laddie knows not where to find the key,
Straightway it shall be given him, if he will ask of me.'

Phasoulaki turned at once: 'Where is it?' he said; 'give me the key.'

Then the little bird with its beak took out from among the feathers on its breast a little golden key, and dropped it into Phasoulaki's hand. 'Take the silver cup,' it said, 'and drink the water, but keep it in your hand, so that the Moor knows not of it,' and flying round the hanging cup it undid with its beak the three knots which bound it by the three chains hanging upon the three branches of those three trees.

But Phasoulaki hastened to unlock the padlock with the key, and immediately the marble slid on one side and the fountain opened at the same moment, when the silver cup fell down.

Instead of catching it in his hands the cup dropped into the middle of the fountain, right down with a splash into its depths. The bird was frightened and flew away, and Phasoulaki for a moment stood speechless, when out of the midst of the fountain rose the figure of a Moor with a grinning face, showing his white teeth, and wearing the silver cup upon the top of his head.

'Good-day, little master,' he cried; 'I thank thee for the silver cup thou hast given me. Come down to my abode, and I will repay thee for the favour,' and before Phasoulaki could speak or escape from the Moor, he had seized him in his arms and was about to descend with him into the fountain.

'Don't be afraid,' he called out when he saw how the child trembled; 'I will do thee good. Fill thy hand with water, and straightway thy palms shall become filled with sequins.'

'Sir Moor, I do not want sequins; I only want a little water for myself and my sheep to drink,' said Phasoulaki timidly.

'Thou hast no longer any sheep,' said the Moor.

'How so? They are sitting there up above in the shade, and all athirst.'

'Let us go and see,' said the Moor, and they both went together, when the poor boy saw indeed that all his sheep were turned into stones—the white sheep being white and the black sheep black stones; and when he saw this he sat down and began to cry.

THE ENCHANTED FOUNTAIN 83

'What can I say to my father? How can I go home without the sheep?'

The Moor stood looking on with folded hands, grinning and showing his white teeth.

In the midst of his tears Phasoulaki saw the golden bird draw near to him, and observed that she went to the fountain, and with her beak locked up the marble after she had replaced it; after which, taking out the key, she flew and perched on a bough over the boy's head, saying: 'Take the key, good child; the lid is fastened, and the Moor must remain outside,' and placed the key in his hand, which Phasoulaki hid in his bosom. The Moor, when he saw what had happened, laughed no more, but began to weep.

'Oh, my prince!' he cried, 'open the lid, and I will do whatever you wish.'

'Make all my sheep which you have bewitched and turned into stones alive again,' said Phasoulaki.

The good Moor did as he was told, and the lifeless stones began to kick and bleat, and rose to their feet.

'What else dost thou want, my prince?'

'Give my sheep water.'

Then the Moor caressed by turns the branches of the plantain tree and they bent down, and fresh drops of dew ran from their leaves like rain and filled the dry trough, and the sheep began to drink.

'What else?' said the Moor.

'I want drink for myself.'

Then the Moor took the cup from his head, and breathing upon it three times, filled it with fresh water and gave it to the boy.

Upon this the golden bird from amid the trees called out: 'Thou hast drunk of the ever-living water and art wise, touch him once on his black mouth and once on his black forehead.'

Phasoulaki lost no time, but jumped on a stone in order to reach him, and gave one slap of the hand on the brow and another on the mouth of the Moor, and immediately he remained there where he stood, a black stump, burnt but still smoking. No one would have known that it had ever been a man.

Phasoulaki then gathered his sheep together and went home, but he was much afraid on account of all that had occurred in that enchanted place. The bird went with him, and as soon as they arrived, perched on an apple tree by the gate.

As soon as the father came back from the country, the child began to tell him of all that had happened to him. He listened with much attention, and his countenance showed great joy. At last Phasoulaki said: 'How is this, father; instead of being angry, thou showest great joy, and by disobeying thine advice I was very nearly being lost myself, as well as losing my flock?'

'No,' replied the father; 'thou didst not disobey me. It was decreed that all that has happened should come to pass at the appointed time, but I knew not that it would come to pass through thee. Where is the golden bird?'

'I don't know, father; but I guess that it is outside on the apple tree.'

The father opened the door: 'Come hither, Prince,' he cried, 'and I will set you free.'

The bird flew down and perched on his knee, and the father, after gently fondling it, pulled out two golden feathers from its wings, when immediately the bird became a Prince in golden raiment, and the two feathers were changed into a golden sword and a golden scabbard.

Phasoulaki bent his knee before him, but the Prince embraced him, and kissing him, said: 'I owe it to thee that I am released from the Moor's enchantments; I will make thee my brother, and we will live together. The key which thou holdest is mine; let us go to my palace. Come, and thou too, father.'

The three then went together, and the Prince opened the fountain, when out of its midst rose a marble palace, with gardens and everything that is beautiful. This was his own palace, which had been submerged by the Moor's magic.

As the iron gates of the palace swung back two women with gold-embroidered garments and crowns on their heads came out. One was old with white hair, and the other was very fair. The elder was the Queen and the mother of the Prince, and the younger was his only sister, the Princess. These had both been made Nereids at the bottom of the fountain, and now that they were released were women again.

The Prince embraced them, and they all three wept for joy. As soon as they found that they owed everything to Phasoulaki, they could not find words enough wherewith to thank him.

They took him into the palace along with his father, and gave him the fair Princess for his wife.

And Phasoulaki = the little bean — grew and became strong and large.

Outside the beautiful palace there remained a blackened burnt log, which was always smoking — that log was the Moor.

THE PARROT'S LANGUAGE

 BEAUTIFUL green parrot that was shut up in a golden cage had learnt to speak man's language, and was so delighted on account of it that she ever afterwards disdained the language of birds.

One day the maid left the door of the cage open, and the parrot flew out and took a flight through a neighbouring wood, but she lost her way, and not knowing by what road to return, she addressed a sparrow whom she met thus: 'Excuse me, sir, but can you tell me——' She did not finish her sentence, for the sparrow flew directly away, because he did not understand the language in which the parrot spoke.

Then she asked a blackbird, but he turned away, for he understood nothing of the parrot's speech, for the parrot spoke with the tongue of men, and did not condescend to speak in the tongue of birds.

Then a magpie came along, and the parrot spoke to her. Instead of flying away the magpie came close to her to look at her face, and then began to laugh and shout, 'Kra-a! Kra-a! Just come and see this strange bird. It isn't a man and yet it talks like a man; it is a bird, and hasn't got a bird's voice.'

All the birds in the wood, when they heard this, came and surrounded the parrot. She was quite confused, being thus in their midst, and could not say another word. Night was coming on, and she was afraid to pass it in the wood, and besides she was hungry, not having eaten anything all day. She therefore put aside all her pride and conceit and said, in the language of birds, what she wanted.

When the birds heard her speak like themselves, they all began to jeer her, and no one evinced any inclination to show her the way. There was a good dove among them, however, who pitied her, and conducted her back to her home.

But through the trouble and mortification of that day the parrot became melancholy—she would not eat, and in less than a week she died.

THE PRINCE AND HIS SISTER

WO royal children—brother and sister—were left orphans before they were ten years old. Their aunt, a sister of the late King their father, became guardian to them both and ruled the kingdom until the Prince should grow up and become King.

This woman was a witch and a magician, and she was resolved to become Queen herself; and with this idea she sought out some way whereby she could rid herself of the Prince and his sister.

She knew a thousand tricks of magic. She used to go by night to a dark cave and bring down the moon's rays from heaven, and assemble all the owls and bats around, and did whatever she willed, were it good or evil, by means of her arts.

When the children grew up and the Prince was eighteen and the Princess sixteen years old, the aunt saw that she had no more time to lose, and she determined upon the very next day to put her bad intentions into effect. By her arts she had discovered that if she attempted the lives of the children she would lose her own directly after their deaths, and thus sacrifice all hopes of reigning herself. So upon the day after his eighteenth birthday she said to the Prince: 'Before thou art made King, my child, thou shouldst go round the world and see different countries and different kingdoms. All things are ready for thy departure; go, and when thou returnest in safety, then shalt thou become the King.'

The Prince heard these words of his aunt and thought them excellent. He was only sorry on account of leaving his sister, but he kissed and embraced her, and kissing his aunt's hand also, he mounted his gold-caparisoned charger and, followed by his suite, took his leave.

His aunt had taken care to put among his suite a very bad man who was her own trusted tool, to whom she had imparted her secret orders that he should so manage that the Prince would never return.

The very day that the Prince left, whilst his poor sister was sorrowing in her chamber alone, and weeping bitterly, her aunt the Regent entered, and approaching her softly, sprinkled her with some water out of a black vase which she held in her hand, when the Princess immediately turned into marble.

As she was quite white, her golden hair also without any difference becoming as white as that of a marble statue, no one could know otherwise, nor could imagine that it had ever been a living body, but would have thought that it was the work of some very eminent sculptor.

The Regent rejoiced greatly when she saw her success, and shutting the door of the chamber, locked it and took away the key.

The next morning it was announced to the whole State that the Princess had died suddenly. She was very much lamented, because she was not only beautiful but very compassionate. The Regent put on black and held her handkerchief to her eyes when she led the way to see the corpse. The body was entirely covered over with a pall, and no one could see the dead Princess. Many silently murmured upon this account, but no one dared to say anything aloud, because the Queen Regent had ordered it to be so.

The shrouded body was therefore

buried in the grave which had been dug for it, the tomb was covered with flowers, and the army fired off a hundred cannon.

A year passed away. Upon the anniversary of the death of the poor Princess, the Queen, her aunt, announced that she had loved her so much that she had ordered a skilful artist to make a marble statue of her, which would that very day be placed in the hall of the palace, when every one was invited to see it. Everything was done as she had commanded, and a vast concourse of people assembled to see the petrified Princess. With one voice all admired the sculptor who had so successfully made a marble figure an exact similitude of the living, for no one knew that it was indeed the very Princess herself, whom the magic arts of the witch her aunt had thus turned into stone.

We will now speak of the Prince. When he left his country he went journeying on for days, for months, nay, for years. He visited countries and kingdoms untold; he went to the very end of the world, to a place where for six months in the year it is broad day, and the other six months dark night. As there was then nothing more to see, he began his homeward journey. It was at this time that the wicked man whom the Queen had sent with him managed one night to separate him from the rest of his suite, in order, as he said, to tell him a secret, and whilst he was yet talking, the Prince's eyes were struck by a flash of lightning, which the witch-Queen had given into his possession for that purpose, and he was blinded; he was then pushed down a shelving rock, and cast into a deep hollow, where a few rolls of bread were thrown to him to eat.

When this bad man returned to his companions he said: 'The Prince is destroyed.'

'Can this be so?'

'He is destroyed—a dragon carried him off and devoured him.'

His lying words were believed, and they all returned homewards, bitterly lamenting the terrible loss of their beloved Prince.

The Prince was left quite blind at the bottom of that deep trench, where he could hardly turn himself round, for the earth where he had struck it in falling had rolled over. He did not know what to do, and sat down in despair. It did not affect him so much that he would possibly die, far from his country, in that desolate place, but the thought that his sister had only him in the world to look to, and that he should never return to her, overcame him. He did not know then how much his sister had suffered from her wicked aunt, nor did he understand that it was she who had also blinded himself; he thought his companions had betrayed him for the purpose of robbery—to gain possession of his horse and his golden weapons.

Suddenly he heard a rustling near him. He stretched forth his hands in his blindness, and got hold of an enormous bird. The bird was frightened and tried to fly away, and carried him along with it hanging on to its neck. Whither it went he could not tell, for it went on flying—flying through the air. At last the bird stopped. The Prince then released it, and the bird flew on by itself. After a little while the Prince heard footsteps approaching, when a voice said roughly: 'Who are you, and what do you want here?'

'I am a blind man, who wants but a little bread and water.'

'Who brought you hither?' said the voice.

'The air brought me.'

'Welcome then—come to my hut.' With those words, trembling bony fingers grasped him by the hand, and led him to a warm place, and seated him on a sealskin.

The Prince could see nothing of his surroundings; if he could, he would surely have trembled for fear, as this was the hut of an old witch, and she had all her enchantments near her. She gave the Prince some water in a cup that was made from a lion's bone, and bread of wild barley baked in an oven upon a snake's skin, and sat herself down near him.

'Prince! Prince! shall I send thee back to thy country?'

The astonished Prince cried: 'How dost thou know me, lady?'

'I know thee. I saw it written in the stars that thou wouldst come here, blinded by the arts of thine aunt, the Queen.'

The Prince was much excited when he heard these words.

'My aunt! Why should my aunt do this?'

'Listen, and you will learn what now thou knowest not.'

Then the old witch told him all that had happened since he left the palace; how his sister had been turned into marble, and had been declared to be dead; and how her aunt had buried a pretended body instead of hers, and had also placed her in the hall of the palace.

As soon as the Prince heard what had happened to his sister he sprang from his seat: 'And is it then decreed that my unhappy sister shall for ever remain a marble statue, and that I am always to be blind?'

'No, my son; I will save you both. If your aunt is a sorceress, I am more powerful than she, and my skill can render her skill of no effect. Thy sister shall come to life again, and thou shalt see the light once more, and become King over thy country.'

'How can this be? tell me, lady. How hast thou the knowledge and power to accomplish this?'

'It is decreed that thy sister shall

live when the hands of her brother clasp her again. It is decreed that thine eyes shall be opened when thy sister's lips shall kiss thee. I have said, and it shall be so.'

After the Prince had slept a short time and was rested, the witch awoke him, and put on him a pair of iron slippers. Then she brought a dog, which was tied with an iron chain, and gave one end of it to the Prince: 'Thou hast a long journey to make, and as thou art not able to see, the dog shall go with thee. Follow him, and fear not. Farewell!'

After saying this the sorceress became mere vapour and vanished before the Prince was even able to thank her.

He started, however, the dog going before and he following after. He walked and walked so far that the iron shoes became as thin as paper. A little more, and they would have been full of holes. At last they came to a part where the Prince heard a language which he recognised.

'Bah! a tired blind man and a dog,' said one.

'The poor creature is going to the palace, that they may take pity on him,' said another.

Then the Prince knew that he was in his own country, and that the dog was going straight to the palace. With lighter footsteps he ascended the steps that led into the palace hall.

The Queen was standing near a high window looking out, and her art told her directly who it was. She knew that if he embraced the statue the Princess would return to life, and that all her magic would fail. She therefore cried out: 'Drive out that blind beggar; he will soil the marble.' Five or six soldiers hastened to him, but not before he had reached the marble statue and clasped his petrified sister.

Immediately she came to life. She

sprang up as if she had just before laid down to sleep.

When the soldiers saw it they were dumfounded, and the swords dropped from their hands.

'My brother—my dear brother!' cried the Princess, as soon as she recognised the blind man, 'what has happened to thee?' And she threw herself upon him, and kissed him, whilst the tears fell from her eyes.

Her lips had hardly touched him when his blind eyes opened, as with a flash of light. The sorceress Queen, when she saw this, fell from the high window—the earth opened where she fell, and the dark chasm swallowed her.

THE CUP OF TEARS

A. Kourtidos

TIMOLEON was ill, very ill; his body was so wasted away that he was nothing but skin and bone; his face had become as white as a wax taper. Oh, it was piteous to see him!

One night he was in great danger—the doctor himself had said so; his mother sat by his bedside near him, and held his burning hand. It was past midnight, but the unhappy mother hung over her child. Suddenly in his delirium he woke up from a heavy sleep, then he turned towards his mother, and, as if he feared something, he clasped her convulsively, and laying his head down upon her knees went to sleep.

And he saw a dream.

It appeared to him that he went up to heaven, and that an angel with a beautiful face and with two large white wings opened a great door and beckoned him in. Timoleon went in and found himself in a magnificent room. The floor was covered with carpets embroidered with real flowers; on the walls there were painted birds, but they were real ones, and they warbled each in their place. Opposite the door there was a golden throne, ornamented by thousands of little angels in pearls, emeralds, and rubies; and strange it was, but these angels moved their wings, and filled the room with a soft light, which floated through it. And on the throne—oh! on the throne sat God,—God Himself, whose countenance gave forth as much light as that of thousands of suns, and on account of this Timoleon could not look up, but from afar he heard the voices of the angels who sang His glory, and their voices were so sweet, and the hymn which they sang was so moving, that Timoleon, transfixed with amazement, stood still in the place where he first found himself. Never had he imagined such things.

Suddenly the angels ceased, and a voice from the throne said: 'Timoleon, come hither. I am God thy Father.'

And Timoleon, his heart throbbing within him, drew nearer.

The light which emanated from the face of God was not like that of the sun, because then he could not have borne it, but the light which he saw, although greater, was more pleasant. It seemed to him as though it shed light into his soul.

Timoleon approached the throne of God.

'Timoleon, my son,' said the voice,

'thou art sick and like to die, but dost thou see this cup (he showed him a golden cup)? if thou canst find any one who will fill this with tears, then thou shalt not die.'

Timoleon began to tremble. Who would weep so much for him as to fill that cup in order to save him?—not he himself could shed so many tears, therefore he must die.

Die! Ah, he did not wish to die —he did not wish to be wrapped in a winding-sheet and to be carried off amid psalmodies to be laid in a grave, and all to go away and leave him alone with the dead in the cemetery. He was afraid—afraid. And in his despair he said: 'No one will be found in the whole world who will shed so many tears to save me!'

'The cup—where is the cup?' cried an agonised voice suddenly at the door, and at that moment there rushed into the room a woman, who seemed beside herself, with dishevelled hair and stretching out her hands towards the throne of God.

Timoleon shivered when he heard that voice, for it was well known to him. He raised his head and saw the woman through his tears.

It was his mother, and she held in her hands the golden cup, and wept—and wept! The tears ran like pearly rains; they flowed—and flowed. And when would they cease? An endless fount seemed to come from her heart, which was full of love and tears; the cup was filled—it overflowed the brim—and yet they did not cease; they fell on to the carpet, and were so burning that they withered the flowers which were embroidered on it. Oh, how many more tears had his mother to give for Timoleon!

The living birds that were on the walls of God's chamber ceased their lovely warbling, and the pearl, emerald, and ruby angels of the throne moved their wings no more. All were motionless at that mother's wonderful love.

But the mother's heart was fearful lest what she had done was not enough to save her child, and she knelt down, as she gave back the cup to God, and in an agitated voice cried out her maternal anguish: 'Save, save my child, O God, and take my life instead!'

'Thy child is saved,' answered God; 'and thou shalt live to see him great and good; thy tears have saved him; if thou hadst not loved him so much he would have died.'

And then the mother rushed to him, and taking Timoleon in her arms, went out of the room, and as she passed along, the angels out of respect drew back on either side.

On their way she clasped him fervently to her breast, and tears fell upon his face, and as she kissed him she whispered softly, 'My dear, dear child.'

Timoleon also embraced his good and loving mother, who had not left him to die, and kissed her with tears of joy and gratitude, whispering 'Mother—mother——'

He awoke.

.   .   .   .   .

The sun had risen, the birds were singing sweetly upon the trees in their garden, and the flowers were shedding abroad the early morning fragrance. A ray of sunshine had shot across the bed where Timoleon was lying, awakened him. He was still embraced by his mother.

'Oh, what a strange dream was that which I have seen! Was it—was it a dream?'

If it were a dream, why, when he awoke, did he see that his mother was embracing and bending over him, looking at him with a glance full of inexhaustible love, and weeping—weeping—as boundlessly as there in the house of God. Was it a dream? and had not his mother's tears saved him from dying? And yet, oh, joy! He was conscious of an unaccustomed fresh feeling in his body, he felt it lighter, just as if the bad illness which had weighed him down had flown away, and he thought that a sweet voice spoke to his heart: 'Thou shalt get well, Timoleon; thou shalt not die.'

When the doctor came after a little while and examined him again and again, he rose with joy and said to the mother: 'Thy child is saved.'

The mother then embraced Timoleon afresh, and tears of joy fell upon his face as she whispered softly, whilst she kissed him: 'My dear, dear child.'

Then Timoleon thought of his dream, and of the words which God had said to his mother.

'Thy child is saved; thy tears have saved him; if thou hadst not loved him so much he would have died,' and he kissed his mother passionately, and pressed his little lips against hers, and from the depths of his heart, in a voice of the greatest tenderness, he said to her who had twice given him his life: 'Mother, I thank thee.'

TWO LITTLE BOOTS

A. Kourtidos

I

N the middle of an alley stood two small wooden huts. One of them had been hired a short time previously by a family consisting of a father, mother, and two sons. The other had been occupied for many years by an old widow and her daughter. In the centre of the alley there was a little round garden, surrounded by flower beds; its flowers smelt very sweetly, and scented the whole alley, as if they were desirous of thus expressing their gratitude to the young girl who watered and took care of them.

The two boys were named Eteokles and Ajax. The one was nine years old, the other seven. They had also a great love of flowers. One can imagine, therefore, with what delight they observed that there was a corner near their house where they could cultivate them. They took an old shovel to serve for a spade, and began to dig up the earth.

This corner of the alley became by degrees quite a little field-plot. Eteokles dug and dug; but whilst he prosecuted his digging with energy, he seemed to find some obstruction beneath the earth. So he set to work with his hands, and at last brought forth two little old boots—worn out and mouldy from the damp.

'Two boots!' shouted Eteokles with surprise, and, throwing down his shovel, he took them up in his hands.

'Who could have put them there?' said Ajax.

'They must have been planted in

order to grow,' answered Eteokles laughing.

'No, my boys, they were buried.'

The old neighbour said these last words. She was sitting on the threshold of her door, with her spectacles on her nose, and knitting socks. She had seen with a smile with what fervour the boys had been digging their little plot of ground, which a child of five years could have crossed in one step.

'They were buried?' cried the boys with some uneasiness, as if there was something uncanny in the word.

'Yes; a little girl buried them.'

As the boys regarded the old woman with eyes filled with curiosity, and with mouths open with surprise, she said: 'If you like, I will tell you the story of those boots.'

The boys looked again at the strange little boots, which even had a story belonging to them, just as if they had been an old statue which had been dug out of the ground, and ran up to the old woman: 'Yes—yes—do tell us——'

'The story?'

The old woman laid down the ball of thread upon her apron, and settling the spectacles anew upon her nose, whilst she still went on knitting, she began to tell the tale of the boots, with some show of emotion, perhaps because of the affecting little story that she was about to relate, or because she was thinking of the old days when she was a schoolkeeper and was surrounded by the cheerful heads of children, whilst her school was all a-hum with childish voices, as though it had been a hive, as she was teaching so many good things to those little angel faces around her.

'These little boots,' said the old woman, 'were at one time the joy and comfort of a poor girl. The most beautiful toy, the most handsome garment would never have caused such emotions, nor filled a heart with so much happiness. The glances we cast upon things do not rest long upon them; if they did remain, you might have seen that nothing was ever looked at with so much love or was loved so faithfully and so constantly as that pair of little boots, which you now see are worn out and mouldy.'

The old woman paused. Both the boys—one on each side of her—looked at her attentively.

'But I must begin from the beginning,' she said, after a little.

And, looking at the needles and the sock in her apron, she began.

II

'A shoemaker in Eolus Street had just made two little boots; they were beautiful—very beautiful; they were of soft leather, and had little holes in front with nice fastenings.

been an old statue which had been dug out of the ground, and ran up to the old woman: 'Yes—yes—do tell us——'

'The story?'

The old woman laid down the ball of thread upon her apron, and settling the spectacles anew upon her nose, whilst she still went on knitting, she began to tell the tale of the boots, with some show of emotion, perhaps because of the affecting little story that she was about to relate, or because she was thinking of the old days when she was a schoolkeeper and was surrounded by the cheerful heads of children, whilst her school was all a-hum with childish voices, as though it had been a hive, as she was teaching so many good things to those little angel faces around her.

'These little boots,' said the old woman, 'were at one time the joy and comfort of a poor girl. The most beautiful toy, the most handsome garment would never have caused such emotions, nor filled a heart with so much happiness. The glances we cast upon things do not rest long upon them; if they did remain, you might have seen that nothing was ever looked at with so much love or was loved so faithfully and so constantly as that pair of little boots, which you now see are worn out and mouldy.'

The old woman paused. Both the boys—one on each side of her—looked at her attentively.

'But I must begin from the beginning,' she said, after a little.

And, looking at the needles and the sock in her apron, she began.

II

'A shoemaker in Eolus Street had just made two little boots; they were beautiful—very beautiful; they were of soft leather, and had little holes in front with nice fastenings.

'This pair of boots was very handsome. Many passers-by stopped for a moment and looked at them, and then went on their way—for the boots were in the midst of a large glass window where there were boots of every size and shape. Each one looked out for that which suited her,—the young lady for a pair of boots with high heels, that looked as if they were ready to dance; the old lady, like myself, for a pair of easy broad shoes which have made bold to think themselves ready to tell you a tale; the children looked out for a pair which, according to their opinion, were suitable for their feet to jump and bound in—for each was in its own place—they outside the glass and the boots within.

'One day a poor woman with very old and threadbare garments passed. She led by the hand a little girl, and the first thing which the child noticed was that beautiful pair of boots; then she turned and looked at her own, which were very, very large, so that besides holding one little foot, each could almost have held another; when she walked she had to drag them after her—they were full of holes and quite spoiled; her look then turned back again to the boots in the window, and she regarded them earnestly, for she longed to have them. Poor little thing! She had so set her heart upon them that she could not understand why her mother pulled her by the hand to go on. As they went away the little girl, with her finger in her mouth, looked back at them, and when she was hardly able to see them any longer she gave them one look—oh, what a look!—as if to bid good-bye to what she loved so much—so much.

'After a little while an open carriage stopped before the bootmaker's, and a grand lady and a little girl of seven years old, with fair plaited hair, stepped out and went into the shop. The bootmaker took the beautiful little boots out of the window, the child put them on with great impatience, and her old ones were rolled up in a newspaper. They then re-entered the carriage, the coachman whipped up the horses, and the carriage wheels rolled quickly forward till they stopped at the door of a large house in Stadium Street, before which they descended.

'The little girl, who you understand clearly must be the lady's daughter, was called Emerald. As soon as Emerald got into the hall she began to run and jump and skip for joy. The boots themselves looked around with amazement. What a hall it was!—all of marble! and so bright that any one could see his face in it; and what a staircase! with those large marble stairs, the little boots would make glad this staircase with their echoes.

'Emerald ran up the middle of it, and skipping merrily entered the drawing-room.

'The boots had begun to have a very good opinion of themselves when they had found that they were admired by so many whilst they were in the bootmaker's window, and they then thought themselves too good to go into a poor house; but now that they saw those carpets, whose softness seemed to be caressing them; when they saw the large golden mirrors, which showed them out as if they were in another imaginary drawing-room which reflected them; when they saw the many easy-chairs, the ebony pianoforte with its ivory keys, and all the other beautiful things, they remained almost in a state of ecstasy. In what kind of palace did they find themselves? Were these things real? What happiness! And so great was the bewilderment caused by their delight that, in order to breathe the better, they loosened the buttons which fastened them. Emerald after a while observed this, and fastened them again, but without imagining what emotions were being aroused around her feet.

'Oh, how happy the little boots were then! They would have liked to live so for ever in the midst of that brilliant circle, and to have always inhaled the sweet perfume of wealth in that scented mansion.

'But on the next day this thought struck them: No one ever made any remark about *them*; they heard no one say: "What beautiful boots!" only, "How beautiful *she* is!"

'"How is this?" the boots said to themselves; "no one takes any trouble to notice how lovely we are, and the only praise they bestow is on the pretty feet of little Emerald."

'This displeased them. And at night, when Emerald took them off, they were left outside the door of her little bedroom, where they stayed the whole night, lonely and melancholy and in the dark. And in the morning a servant woke them in a rough way out of a sweet sleep and took them down into the kitchen to be cleaned, where they heard all the vulgar talk of the servants and saw the cook washing up the dishes, and where they were thrown among a heap of other boots and shoes, who looked at them strangely and made a jest of their small size. There were two soldier's boots with spurs on them, and there were two others so gigantic that every morning as soon as they saw them they could not help laughing out heartily. The thick hand of the servant, however, hurt them, rubbing them every day hard with a brush in order to blacken them.

'Notwithstanding these troubles they forgot them when morning came and Emerald put them on and went into the drawing-room or down into the hall, or ran long the narrow garden walks, which were strewn with small stones and bore the smell of the flowers; when they saw the foliage of the trees, and heard the breeze murmuring among the leaves.

III

'Two months had passed since they came to that house, but oh, how things had changed! Now they were sad and sorrowful, because Emerald regarded them with complete indifference—she threw them on one side. For it is impossible for any one to imagine their grief and their agony when Emerald's mother, after looking well at them one day, said: "Emerald, after dinner we must go and order some boots."

'And Emerald was glad, and she went running into the hall, as she was accustomed to do when she was pleased, with a little jump like a kid's at the end, and said to a maid: "Rose, mamma tells me that after dinner we are going to order some new boots."

'This word "new" tore the heart of those others as though it had been a knife. If the bootmaker, when he was making them, had let slip his knife it would not have pained them so much.

'From that moment all looked dark. When, after dinner, it was necessary to go in the carriage they thought that they must have expired on the road. How things appeared on that first journey home from the bootmaker's, and how did they appear now! They trembled when they got to the shop, as the bootmaker took them off Emerald's feet in order to take her measure. Then they turned and looked around them. Oh, that glass window! It was there, in that place, where now there were others, that they remembered the kindling looks of the children, the expressions of wonderment, and the smiles which showed their love for them; especially they remembered the pathetic glances of a little girl whose poor mother drew her away from the window, and who turned to look again and again. Ah—and now! So much were they affected by these remembrances that the little boots never knew that Emerald had put them on again, and that they were again in the carriage on their way home.

'A few days afterwards they again went to the bootmaker's; Emerald put on her new boots, and the bootmaker brought her the others wrapped up in a newspaper. That newspaper seemed like a winding-sheet. When they reached home Emerald gave them to a maid, who threw them into a corner, and Emerald went down into the hall dancing and skipping and running like one who was very fortunate. Oh, what more! the happy days were gone, now only misfortune and distress were left behind; no longer would they feel the gliding, the caressing warmth of those little feet. What could they do now—who knows? What all unhappy ones do,—they would fall down, perhaps, into some cellar, and there, in dark and mouldy damp, they would pass the rest of their miserable days. They trembled with dread, and their heart beat like a clock—Tik-tak, tik-tak.

IV

'But what was taking place in the house which caused so much commotion? They had a wash.

'Now when they had a wash, a poor woman who had formerly been a servant in the house when the lady of that house was a girl living in her mother's home, came to do the washing. She had married a workman at the powder factory, which is, as you know, a little outside Athens, and she lived very happily with her husband until one dreadful day a light caught the powder, and the factory and all the workmen were blown up. Oh, alas, alas! not even the scattered and mangled remains of the poor man could be gathered together in order to give them burial. And thus she was left a widow with an orphan girl. Her old mistress employed her to wash in order to find an opportunity of giving her a few pence.

'The little girl Anthoula was the same age as Emerald. She was a beautiful child, with very large chestnut eyes, which had a great deal of feeling in them, and gave one the impression that they had something to say. She had a lovely face, which looked still more engaging on account of the orphan's black clothes which she wore; whilst on her feet she had a pair of large, old boots full of holes.

'Emerald looked at Anthoula, and her glance fell down to her feet. For once she became melancholy, then suddenly her eyes sparkled, and she ran to her mother.

'She whispered some words in her ear, turning very red, casting meanwhile very significant looks at Anthoula, when her mother, instead of answering anything, took her in her arms and kissed her many times, and gave her her answer amid kisses. Emerald then ran and brought the old boots, which she held out to Anthoula.

'Anthoula asked permission from her mother by a look; she made a sign to her to receive them, and as she took them her large eyes were suddenly lighted up with the greatest pleasure and surprise—running to her mother, she cried: "Mother, do you know them?"

'"What?"

'"They are those——"

'"Those what?"

'"Those which I saw—that day—and told you of them on the road."

'The boots trembled with delight when they heard those words, as soon as they saw that the kindling look of love which they remembered in the poor girl was hers.

'Ah! she recognised them, old and worn though they were, as a heart that loves faithfully recognises its friend whether in age or misfortune. What a good girl! Would that they could put themselves one upon the right cheek and the other upon the left, and kiss her and kiss her!

'They felt the greatest joy which man can feel when he is expecting a sudden death, and life is granted him.

'"Then we are still loved—we can still live," said the boots over again to reassure themselves. The boots, on account of their emotion, had not noticed the shabby clothes of Anthoula and her mother. But when, in the evening, they noticed their poor room, in which all the furniture was a mattress on a wooden frame, an old table, and two worn-out straw chairs, they were annoyed.

'"What!" they said to each other, "we have fallen low indeed. We have always been accustomed to walk on carpets, on marble, and now we are compelled to walk on these planks, on this earth? They have surely brought us here out of contempt, or for punishment. Alas for all our hopes—alas for all our joy! Such a life—so humble and contemptible; such daily companionship with misery and rags and bits of dry bread is worse than death! We are unfortunate, always unfortunate! It is finished!" they whispered in despair.

'But whilst they were indulging in these mournful ideas, Anthoula asked a neighbour for a little blacking, and blacked and polished them till they shone like a mirror.

'This first experience was not at all displeasing to them; their anger began to pass quickly away, like that of all quick-tempered people. "Let us wait and see," they said; they thought they could put up with things as they appeared, and began to look upon affairs from a different aspect.

'Their fate was not so bad! And, above all, how different was the love of Emerald from that of Anthoula!

'Emerald loved them as something new—as a mere ornament for her feet;

the same as she loved all the new boots which she had worn before them, and would love all that came after them.

'But Anthoula loved them only; they were the only boots which had appealed to her heart; and at the moment when Emerald had driven them far from her, Anthoula had opened her arms to them.

'They no longer had a feeling that they were useless, for now Anthoula had made them useful. Anthoula had become the cause why they should still make their appearance in the world.

'There was not wanting in them therefore some little gratitude towards Anthoula.

'Yes, the room was poor, but every morning they were not the thick hands of a servant, but Anthoula's delicate hands, that polished and caressed them.

'And those large brown eyes of hers

which reflected them more beautifully than gilt mirrors, how happy she made them with her look so full of love and expression! Never, never had they had such a feeling! And at night, whilst Anthoula was asleep, whilst they rested in one corner of the room, why did they think that they got off the floor, although they were motionless in their place, and flew and circled round and round the beautiful head of Anthoula, who was lying on the pillow? Oh! because the good girl saw them there close to her in her dreams and in her sleep.

'Who could have told them that at last, out of black despair, such happiness could have been brought to them. They remembered their past grandeur no more.

'What a beautiful thing is love!

V

'But in this world all things grow old, especially boots, and these boots had much aged, and although they had no teeth to fall out, the little fastenings fell out. They were worn and could no longer run, and instead of jumping, they crawled—crawled; one day they were so sick that they could not get along at all, so Anthoula was very much afraid, and took them to the boot doctor, and he did what he could, and was able to set them upon their feet again, but in a short time they got all wrong once more, and took to their bed; the doctor performed a serious operation on them, and hardly succeeded in restoring them, but the signs of disease were left behind. Anthoula was altogether heart-broken to see how they were drooping, but when they were again really ill and she called in the doctor, he said that doctoring could do no more for them, that no hope was left, and that the patients must die.

'"What from?" asked Anthoula with tears.

' "From old age, little lassie."

'And truly at night the little boots could not stand; they began to expire, but during their death-struggle their looks turned with inexpressible gratitude to the eyes of the good girl who had made them so happy, who had not only loved them, but had made them capable of loving, which is a still greater blessing.

'At four in the afternoon they died.

'Anthoula, who had felt a cold shudder when it was suggested that they were only fit to be thrown in the dust-cart like a putrid cat, went herself into that corner, and kneeling down, dug a hole with her hands, and wept, and——'

'And buried them!' cried the two boys, who had listened all through without saying a word.

'What became of the little girl?'

'She is in the orphanage—her mother is dead.'

'Poor thing!'

. . . . .

The boys went slowly, very slowly, back to their little garden. Without saying a word they understood each other, and took the boots carefully and buried them again in their former tomb at the end of their garden.

The two boys planted flowers and tended and watered them, so that loved and cherished things grew over that grave and scattered around the sweet odours of remembrance.

Such a tomb have the little boots. They are not forgotten, and are still fortunate although dead.

OUR ORPHAN

A. Kourtidos

I

N a narrow road of Athens, just behind the Akropolis, was a little house on the ground-floor. The walls were half crumbled away, and the roof seemed ready to fall in; there was no glass in the windows, and when the wind blew they had to stop the holes with pieces of newspaper to keep out the cold; but when the winter winds blew they came through the many holes in the house, howling in fury, and they could find nothing that would answer to keep out the cold. There was no fire

lighted on the hearth; there was no furniture—none; the wind was therefore free to blow round the naked walls and the bare floor, and the two human beings who lived there shivered with cold.

II

One of those beings was a child—an orphan—hardly ten years old. It was alone in the world; its father and mother, who were poor people, were dead, and it had no other relation except a distant aunt who had pity upon it and took it to her humble dwelling, where they lived together, but she was too wretched herself to feed it properly, so that the miserable orphan—from the trials of those sad bereavements which blight the lives of so many children, from the want of a little love, as the many flowers which wither from the want of a few rays of sunshine—fell sick, and in a short time was unable to go outside to talk and play with the neighbouring children.

It lay upon a wretched straw mattress near the window, so that in the springtime it could see the sun rise in the early morning and set in the evening; it heard the warbling of the swallows which flew about merrily on the opposite roofs; and it could look at a tall tree which was in the little garden of a neighbouring coffee-house.

III

One day a little boy ran down the narrow road, and chancing to give a look at the window, he saw the pale little orphan. As soon as he saw it he felt so sympathetic directly that he held out his hand and gave it the orange which he was carrying. The orphan took it with its thin and bony fingers, and its pale lips smiled. The boy went on his way, but as soon as he got to school he told his companions how the poor child had affected him— the poor child which could not move from its straw mattress. His friends were all kindly children, and they went together and saw it, and not a day passed afterwards without a child going to the window and taking the orphan either fruit or flowers.

None of the children had ever known anything of the orphan before, none of them knew its name, and there was no necessity, for they gave it a much more sympathetic one when they called it *our orphan*. Many a time these good children, instead of buying toys, kept their halfpence in order that they might take something to *their orphan*, and when they heard its sweet, faint, little voice say, 'Thank you,' they were delighted because they had given pleasure to the unhappy orphan.

IV

Time went on, but the children did not forget their orphan.

Autumn came—the swallows sang no more on the opposite roof, the leaves of the large trees had turned yellow, and the sun began to give out no more warmth, for winter was drawing near—all things were changing, but the orphan made no change; it still remained on its straw mattress, pale and fading.

No, no, the orphan had changed too.

V

One of the children went back one day and stood before the window to hand in a little coat which his mother had sent to keep the cold from it, but the orphan did not stretch out its hand to take it; it was no more in its accustomed place on the straw mattress. The boy stooped down and saw a little wooden coffin, and in it the orphan with folded hands and cotton on its mouth; near it a little taper was burning, and the old aunt was weeping; a few withered flowers which a child had left the day before were scattered over its breast.

Ah! the orphan had no need for the

little coat, for it was no longer cold. It had died from poverty, and it was not necessary to wear it in the grave. So the boy took the coat back again, crying. In a little while all the children heard the news and ran to the little chapel, where an old priest read the funeral service.

VI

The children returned from the funeral together; they were very sad: they had lost their little pensioner—their orphan was dead. Some shed tears, and when a passer-by asked the sympathetic child who had brought the coat why he cried, the good boy said sorrowfully, '*Our orphan* is dead!'

A HERO'S STATUE

A. Kourtidos

I

HOW many thousand years I was a piece of marble in Pentelicus I am not able to tell you, because I had not very clear ideas whether I was alive or not; it appeared to me that I had been sleeping, deep, deep down in the bowels of a rock, ever since the creation of the world; the only thing which I can remember like a dream was that day when something with a terrific noise seemed to tear me away and cut me off from the other marble surrounding me. Afterwards I learnt that I had been blasted by a charge of gunpowder, for I fell into a deep sleep again, and do not know what took place until I gradually began to awake, when I found myself in a sculptor's workshop.

One day I heard a low noise—tsik-tsak, tsik-tsak—made by an iron tool—a chisel, and little bits of marble seemed to be falling on me. After a time I became conscious that I had a head, a body, hands, and feet, but I felt all these to be very heavy and torpid.

The chisel went on its work—tsik-tsak, tsik-tsak—and little bits like scales seemed to fall away from me; from the moment that I became conscious of a body, it seemed as if there was something like a wall before me, and it oppressed me; the chisel cleared it away and my chest became free; my mouth appeared to be stopped up with marble, but the chisel opened it and made me breathe—yes, I breathed with the rapture of a living being who has never breathed since the creation of the world; my lids were closed—very heavy, very heavy, but the chisel—tsik-tsak, tsik-tsak—cleared away the stony veil from my eyes.

I was stirred with life from that day; every stroke of the chisel awoke me more and more from my lethargy, and oh, joy, I had not only awoke—I was living! Ah, how happy I was! What a beautiful thing is life! and what a beautiful thing for any one to be as much as possible like man! But yet I had not known it—I—I—was in the midst of shapeless heavy marble, and a sculptor called me forth from thence.

What a wonderful sculptor he was! He was hardly twenty-five years old when he was working on me; you would have thought that he had a fever: his eyes shone; his face was like a living flame; his long hair seemed to tremble with emotion; his head,—oh! you would have thought that something was burning in it. The ideas out of his broad forehead came to his very finger-tips and passed into his chisel; they came to me and were scattered over my whole body, there were flung into my face, into my form, not only bravery, courage, hardihood, and resolution, but also goodness and good feeling.

One day, whilst he was turning me round and round and examining me on every side, it appeared to me that the fire of his looks, the last caresses of his chisel, gave me still more life, made me softer, made my marble limbs more human, and in my left breast I felt conscious of something living, as if with my form of man he had also given me what it wanted—a heart.

And truly, my breast became filled with feelings, and I began to love Greece much, very much, and wished that I could die to see her great and free, and I dreamed of guns and battles, of hills and passes, of conflicts and victory, of Souliotes and chiefs, and the gaining of the banners of the enemy.

On that day, whilst the sculptor was looking at me, after long emotion, he said softly: 'It is in very sooth Markos Botsares[1] himself, Markos Botsares.' Then was this handsome face, with the long hair, in jacket and fustanella,[2] that of Markos Botsares, and has the sculptor taken the feelings of Markos Botsares and put them into my breast?

Oh, I thank thee, I thank thee, sculptor, for the honour thou hast done to a humble block of marble!

. . . . .

II

Now I am no longer in a sculptor's workshop; I am in a great library—the four walls of which are filled with large and gilt-bound books, and the floor is covered with a rich carpet.

[1] The hero of Missolonghi, a Souliote chief.
[2] White cotton skirt, the national costume.

The same day on which they brought me there and stood me by the window, he who had bought me called his two sons into the library, and showing them me, said reverently: 'This is the statue of Markos Botsares, and it is a splendid sculpture.'

The two boys came close to me.

'Look at it and admire it,' said the father with evident emotion; 'this statue is the work, and the last work, of a sculptor, still a young man of only twenty-five years of age, but a great genius, who would have achieved great excellence if he had not met with a terrible misfortune.'

'What has happened to him?' said the elder with anxiety.

'He went out shooting, and his gun exploded and carried away the five fingers of his right hand. If it had only carried away his fingers,' said the father sorrowfully, 'but it has carried away his future—his fame. It has deprived art and Greece of an excellent artist.'

'How sad!' said the elder boy.

'Yes, it is sad,' said the father in a tone of sorrow and enthusiasm combined; 'it is sad because he was a great artist—one of those who give life to the marble, not only life humanly speaking, as of sixty or seventy years, but a life which lasts for thousands of years, like the Hermes of Praxiteles and the Venus of Melos, and now the unfortunate man is obliged to stifle the ideas which are within him, because he can no longer throw them into the marble; but it will not last—no; he is dying by degrees of consumption. What a misfortune!'

The boys were much affected, the elder one especially, who wept.

'Observe,' said the father, approaching me nearer, 'do you not think that he has put motion into the marble? Who that sees that position, that expression of the face, but does not

A HERO'S STATUE

think that it is the very man himself, who, were he here, would despise death and be ready to die for his country like a hero!'

'Yes, yes,' said the younger boy with enthusiasm; 'he looks like a true hero.'

'In this statue,' continued the father, 'there are observable two things in which the ancient Greeks excelled every other nation—art and heroism. They fought at Marathon, but they made the Parthenon; some of us modern Greeks have attained to their heroism but not to their art, and so in this respect we are not yet true Greeks.'

The father left in a little while, but the two boys remained before me and looked at me for a very long while, and then they both went thoughtfully away, and left me alone.

Now that I am alone I can grieve freely on account of the frightful accident which has happened to the sculptor, who made me what I am as it were from nothing, and who by his skill has doubly honoured me because, beside the feelings of Markos Botsares, he has put great ideas into me, and has made me a work of excellence.

Poor artist!

I am very sad, but the two boys come every day and look at me and console me, and whilst they are looking at me I observe that the expression of the elder is like the kindling countenance of the sculptor, and that the heart of the younger has within it those feelings for his country with which the heart of Markos Botsares throbbed, and that when they take leave of me and go away, the elder thinks that the beautiful creations which will one day emanate from his chisel are already smiling upon him, whilst the younger boy thinks that he hears guns, and that he is rushing into the midst of the enemy, and fighting

—fighting as a hero, and dying bravely for his country.

III

Oh, what an honour for me to be thus sculptured! To inspire art and heroism into two children—to make a great sculptor and a great hero for Greece. I, a poor block of marble from the hills.

THE END

Printed by R. & R. CLARK, *Edinburgh.*

www.ingramcontent.com/pod-product-compliance
Lightning Source LLC
LaVergne TN
LVHW061215060426
835507LV00016B/1936